The Sun In Her Soul
Michelle Tran's Magical Vietnamese Fan

Written by Stacy Shaneyfelt
Co-Authored by Michelle Tran
Collaborated With Maxell Nguyen
Illustrated by Joshua Aso

Stacy's dedication:

In addition to magical, talented, gorgeous, and girl power Michelle, I dedicate this book to all of my Asian and Asian American friends, family, students, and parents, from Okinawa, Oklahoma, Pittsburgh, to the Philippines, especially in loving memory of my step-grandma, Araceli Shaneyfelt. I also create it for Vinnie, Alex, Grace, Maxell, Soumountha, and the other special people, especially former students, who have given me constellations of laughs, love, and cultural lessons in life! On a social justice note, please stop the recent hate and crimes against Asians and Asian-Americans worldwide, as well as all other groups. Let's fan ourselves against racism in all forms and spread love!

Michelle's dedication:

I dedicate this book to my family who were never shy of showing me the beauty and richness of my culture and what it means to be a proud Vietnamese-American.

Furthermore, I would like to dedicate this section to Stacy Shaneyfelt who always nurtured my creative spirit and continuously pushed me to think outside of the box. Her lessons will continue to inspire others for lifetimes to come.

Max's Tribute:

I dedicate all of my contributions to people looking to learn more about Vietnamese-American culture and my friends and family who have supported me throughout my life. Additionally, I want to spotlight Stacy Shaneyfelt for pushing me out of my shell and revealing to me the importance of socialization, respect, and empathy for others. I always reference her as the teacher who changed the course of my life.

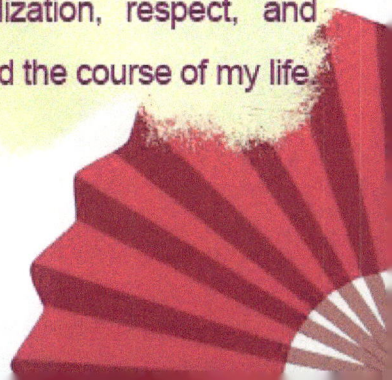

One sunny September school day at Moore West, Michelle Tran zips with such sass, quirk, and zest.

Excited about the cultural show and share today, she carries her panda backpack in a careful way.

Feeling butterflies flutter around,
She enters class with friends abound.
As Anh and the others display such
cool stuff, Michelle frets that hers
isn't quite special enough.

Looking back as a tot, her parents were always so wise. Upon sharing Vietnamese traditions, they dazzled her brown eyes.

For example, her favorite was the paper fan, a treasure for sure. As a special Vietnamese symbol, the quạt giấy will always endure.

Along with her American flag and special flower, Michelle's fan gives her pride and cultural power.

Like a constellation, these objects are precious things: These two unique cultures make her diversity sing!

RIIIIING!!!!

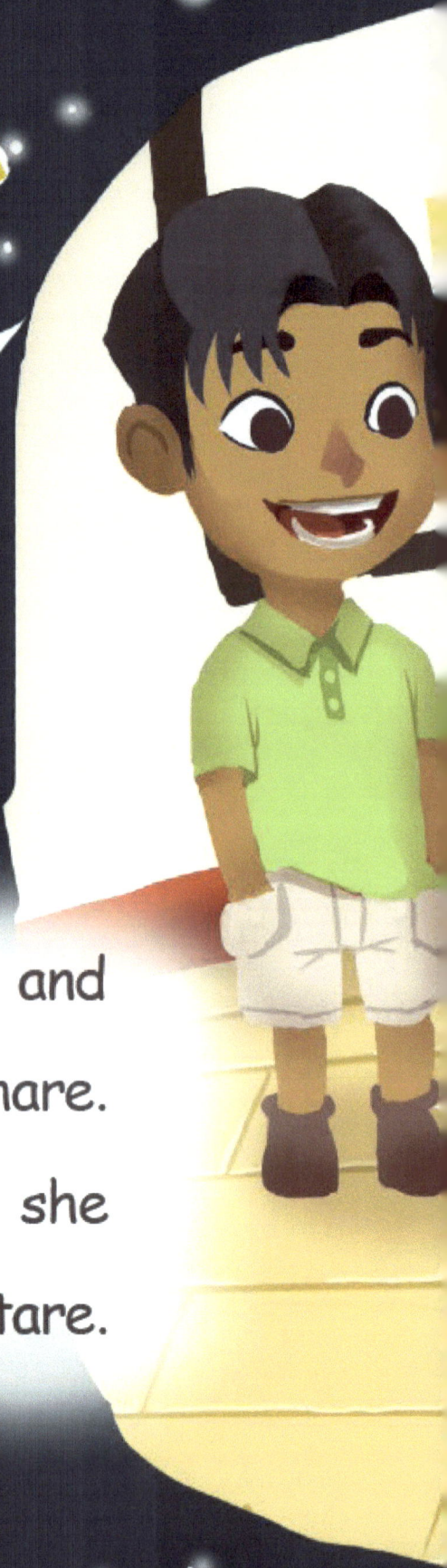

Suddenly, the bell blares, and it's Michelle's turn to share. Standing in the center, she feels everyone smile and stare.

First, she shows a map of Vietnam and each parent's native city.

All the lovely nature, colorful markets, and pagodas look pretty.

Displaying her fan, she talks about its value in her Asian American life.

As the sun in her soul, the fan's constellation of culture beams above strife!

In turn, PJ cheers, "Wow, your fan is super special and unique!" He giggles at his new lobster glow from his head to his feet.

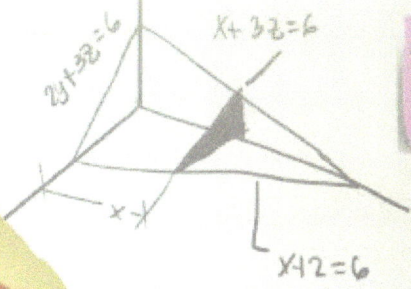

Happily, she adds, "While most Asian fans open more than 180 degrees, Vietnamese fans seem like the sun shines straight into your soul!"

Lovely Adrianna beams like the Oklahoman sun now. She cheers, "These facts are simply wow, wow, wow!"

Next, Molly begs, "Tell about this fan's art, so special and rare!" So Michelle explains Han Nom characters and their special flair: "Check out the amazing script for Heaven, People, and Land. They symbolize prosperity. Moll, please give me your hand!"

In addition, she talks about Do paper, made from silk and bamboo. Max interrupts, "Silk like the worm?" His dance is funky and new!

Bursting with energy, Cassius inquires, "Please talk about colors, so vibrant, special, and bright!" Michelle lets him mix dark reds, blacks, yellows, browns, and violet – all fan colors just right!

Before the final bell, they all share their fans together. There's real magic in the air; a unity that time won't weather.

With sun in her soul, Michelle Tran gives her Vietnamese fan a twirl. Everyone cheers loudly and proudly for this stary-eyed, special girl!

Post-Reading Family Fun, Activities, and Discussions:

1. Virtual Vietnamese Field Trip: Expand your geographical, cultural, and historical knowledge. Go online and locate 4-6 fun facts about Vietnam with a grownup's permission. You may also check out a book about Vietnam from your local library.

2. Rhyme Time: Identify 4-6 pairs of rhyming words in this book. Read them and spell them aloud for speech practice.

3. Culture Jar: Create a culture jar or cup to collect special artifacts, symbols, pictures, and items to celebrate your unique culture or cultures. Ask another person to help you in this dynamic DIY activity!

4. Diversity Rap, Cheer, Poem, or Song: Devise your own song, rap, cheer, poem, or chant about how to accept and honor other genders, races, cultures, religions, disabilities/abilities, and areas of differences.

5. Oklahoman Adventure: Explore culture, history, and geography associated with this Sooner state. Go online with a grownup's permission or visit the local library to learn 4-6 fun facts about Oklahoma.

6. Vocabulary Valor: Jot down 4-6 new words that you've learned from this book. Use context clues to infer the meanings. With an adult's help, consult a dictionary to compare your definition to the real ones. Get vocabulary valor!

7. Show and Tell: In the story, Michelle loved her fan because it was beautiful and rare. Find an item that is special to you and write down why!

_____

_____

_____

8. Zany Zoo: Otis the dog makes a "woof" sound. Can you think of what sounds these animals make?

Pig:

Cow:

Octopus:

Monkey:

Frog:

9. Popcorn Reading: Find a grownup or a friend and try to take turns reading out loud!

10. Get Creative!: Create your own magical fan like Michelle's. Feel free to decorate with your own culture/s, personality, hobbies, favorite colors, etc.

Materials:

- Paper Plate

- Scissors

- Craft Sticks

- Markers

- Paint & Brushes

- Glue

Craft:

1. Cut the paper plate in half.

2. Decorate the half plate. You can just use markers to draw or paint first. If painting both sides, let dry a few minutes before flipping over to paint the other side.

3. Once fully dry, color with markers or other decorations.

4. Glue craft sticks together at one end at about a 90 degree angle. Next, attach to the back of the plate.

5. Let glue dry and then enjoy the magic from your fan!

ABOUT THE AUTHOR

After obtaining her BS in Secondary English Education and MA in English from Slippery Rock University of PA, Stacy embarked on a successful teaching career that spanned public, government, and charter schools in Pittsburgh, PA, Oklahoma City, Norman, OK, and Okinawa, Japan. She proudly earned a 2004 Fulbright-Hays Seminar Scholarship to Thailand and Vietnam from the United States Department of Education, Teacher of the Year in two schools, as well as other teaching accolades. In addition to multicultural and social activism, Stacy now savors sweet moments with her awesome husband, two fierce and fabulous daughters, and three frisky fur babies. Presently working as a virtual freelancer, she enjoys films, travel, coffee, art, cats, and all things mindful!

ABOUT THE CO-AUTHOR

A recent graduate of the University of Central Oklahoma, Michelle holds a Bachelor's of Business Administration in Management Information Systems. Michelle currently serves as a Software Engineer in Oklahoma City where she volunteers for the Oklahoma City Women in Technology chapter and holds a membership in the Society of Women Engineers. As a second generation Vietnamese American, Michelle also volunteers for the Asian Professional Association where she is involved with a podcast to highlight the stories and challenges of Asian Americans in her community. She strives to bridge the gap for Women in STEM careers and hopes to inspire fellow Asian Americans.

Outside of work and volunteerism, Michelle enjoys anything related to fitness from kickboxing to powerlifting. In her spare time, she loves to spend time with her French Bulldog, Otis and her boyfriend, Jack.

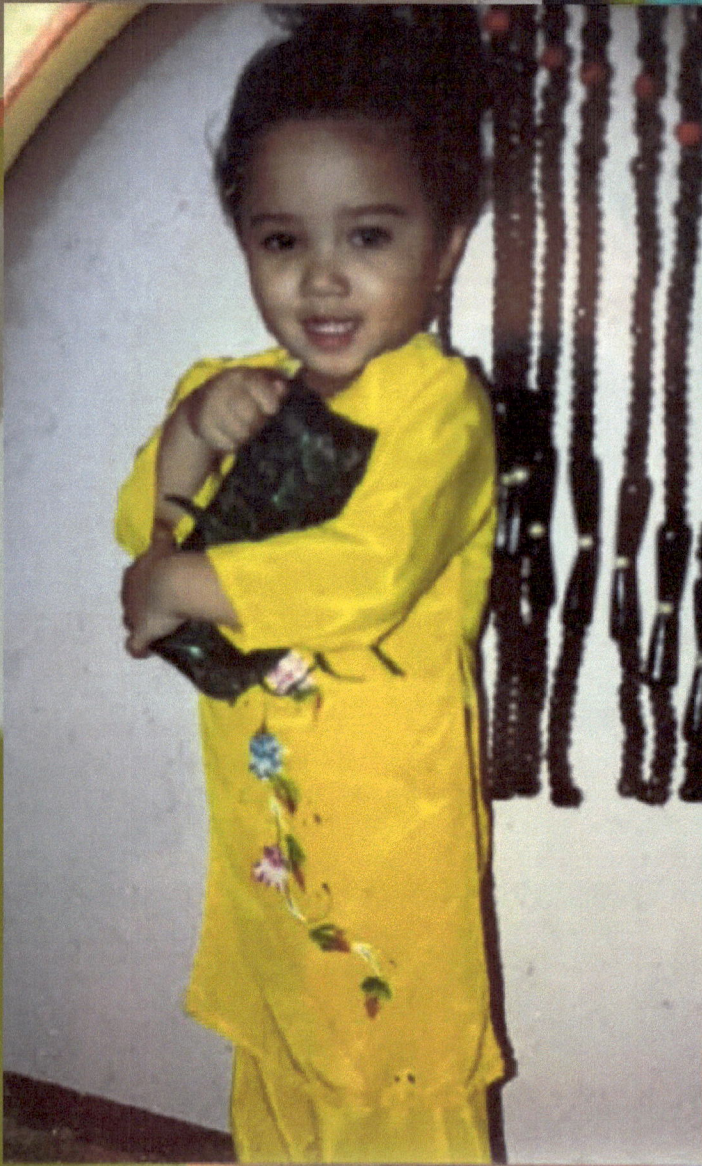

A former and present photo of Michelle Tran and Otis

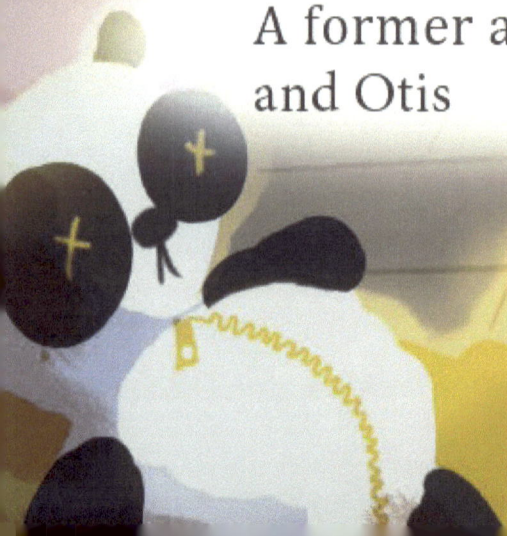

Thank you for buying this book. As a working mom and military spouse, your reviews mean so much to me because I aim to unite global readers through art and literacy. Kindly post a short review on this book's Amazon page. I truly appreciate you for book buzzing with me! If you like this book, then please check out my other buzzworthy offerings at https://www.amazon.com/Stacy-Shaneyfelt/e/B08TVX-7C5X/

www.ingramcontent.com/pod-product-compliance
Lightning Source LLC
Chambersburg PA
CBHW060854270326
41934CB00002B/138